Christmas Trees
COLORING BOOK

Barbara Lanza

DOVER PUBLICATIONS, INC.
MINEOLA, NEW YORK

Featuring thirty-one charming Christmas trees—some realistically rendered, and others formed from abstract patterns and design motifs—this coloring collection is sure to put you in the holiday spirit! The latest edition to Dover's *Creative Haven* series for the experienced colorist, the highly detailed designs allow for experimentation with different media and color technique. Plus, the perforated pages make displaying your finished work easy!

Copyright
Copyright © 2015 by Barbara Lanza
All rights reserved.

Bibliographical Note
Christmas Trees Coloring Book is a new work, first published by
Dover Publications, Inc., in 2015.

International Standard Book Number
ISBN-13: 978-0-486-80390-6
ISBN-10: 0-486-80390-2

Manufactured in the United States by RR Donnelley
80390207   2015
www.doverpublications.com

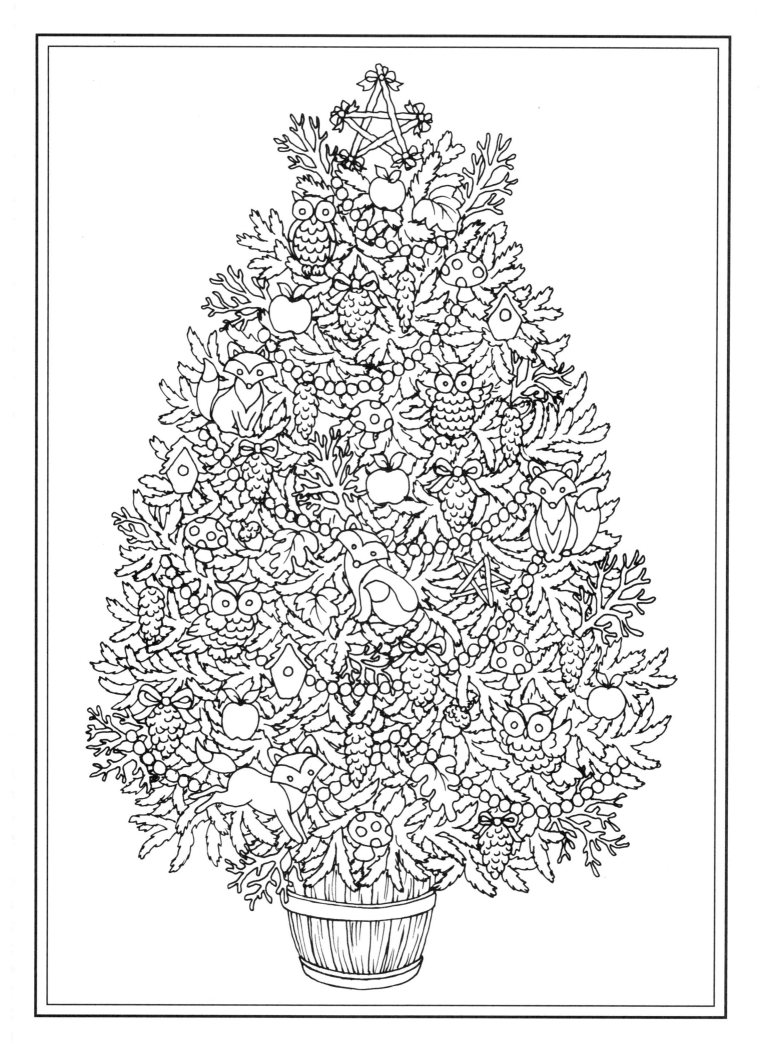